PAWS
AND CLAWS

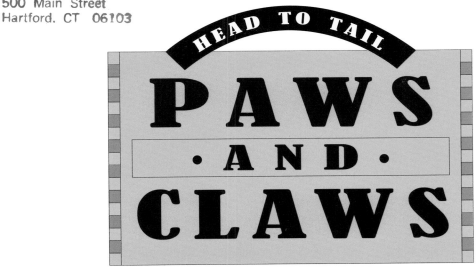

HEAD TO TAIL
PAWS
· AND ·
CLAWS

WRITTEN BY
THERESA GREENAWAY

SCIENTIFIC CONSULTANT JOYCE POPE
ILLUSTRATED BY ANN SAVAGE,
JULIAN AND JANET BAKER

RSVP
RAINTREE
STECK-VAUGHN
PUBLISHERS
The Steck-Vaughn Company

Austin, Texas

Library of Congress Cataloging-in-Publication Data

Greenaway, Theresa, 1947–
Paws and claws / by Theresa Greenaway.
p. cm. — (Head to tail)
Includes index.
ISBN 0-8114-8266-9
1. Foot—Juvenile literature. 2. Hand—Juvenile literature.
3. Claws—Juvenile literature. 4. Animals—Juvenile literature.
[1. Paws. 2. Claws.] I. Title. II. Series: Greenaway, Theresa, 1947– Head to tail.
QL950.7.G76 1995
591.4'9—dc20
94–30730 CIP AC

Editors: Wendy Madgwick and Maurice J. Sabean
Designer: Janie Louise Hunt

Printed in Spain
1 2 3 4 5 6 7 8 9 0 LB 99 98 97 96 95 94

Contents

All About Paws

Paws are an animal's hands and feet. You can tell how an animal moves from its paws. Different kinds of paws mean animals can move in different ways. Some run fast, some can jump or hop. Some climb trees and others swim. Animals also use their paws to hold food, dig, or clean themselves.

▶ **Domestic Cat** Your pet cat has small paws with soft pads. Most of the time a cat walks slowly along the ground. When it hunts, a cat can run really fast. It also uses its paws to clean behind its ears!

▲ **Olive Baboon** Like many other monkeys, baboons groom each other with their hands. They untangle the fur and remove insect pests with their fingers. This keeps their fur clean. It also helps the animals care for each other.

▶ **Meadow Vole** This little vole eats seeds, grass stems, and grain. It sits upright and holds its food in its tiny front paws. This allows it to watch for danger while it is eating.

▼ **Coypu** The coypu lives near rivers and streams in South America. It uses its webbed back feet to help it swim.

▲ **Philippines Tarsier** This little tarsier feeds at night. In the daytime, it climbs into the trees to sleep. It has soft pads on its fingers and toes. These help it cling to the tree trunk.

All About Claws

Take a look at your fingers and toes. Each one has a nail at the end. These nails protect the ends of your fingers and toes. Other animals also have nails. In some they have become strong claws. Claws can help grip the ground or climb a tree. They can also dig a hole or scratch an enemy! In other animals, nails have become hard hooves.

▼ **Domestic Horse** The horse has one large toenail on each foot. This is called a hoof. Horses can gallop very quickly on their tough hooves.

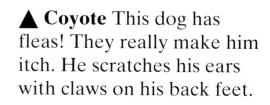

▲ **Coyote** This dog has fleas! They really make him itch. He scratches his ears with claws on his back feet.

◄ Garden Spider The garden spider spins a web of fine silk. Each one of her eight feet ends in three tiny claws. She often walks around on her web. Then she grips the silk threads with these claws.

▼ Red Panda The red panda usually walks on the ground. When it wants to rest, it uses its sharp claws to climb. The red panda likes to sleep on a sunny branch.

◄ Aardvark The aardvark has strong front claws. It uses them to dig into the hard ground to make a home. The aardvark eats termites. It breaks open the termites' nests with its claws.

Fast Movers

A lot of animals can run very fast. Hunters run fast to catch their prey. Hunted animals run fast to escape from them. Some animals live in big groups. These groups, or herds, can run for a long time. Their babies can run soon after being born. Other animals can run very fast for a short distance. They sprint to safety.

▶ **Cheetah** The cheetah can run faster than any other animal. It can reach up to 70 miles (112 km) an hour for a short distance. The cheetah creeps up close to its prey. Then it starts to run.

◀ **Gnu** The gnu (wildebeest) lives in enormous herds. It has two hooves on each foot. Its calves can run along only 30 minutes after they are born. Gnus keep moving to stay away from predators.

◀ **Red Kangaroo** There is little food in the hot, dry parts of Australia. The kangaroos have to travel great distances to find enough to eat. They move along on their big back feet, making long bounds. Each leap is about 13 feet (4 m) long. They can move at 40 miles (64 km) an hour for short distances.

▲ **House Mouse** This small mouse needs a quick sprint to reach the safety of its hole. It moves so fast that it looks just like a blur!

▶ **Impala** Impalas are hunted by many animals. They have to run fast to escape. They can leap up to 30 feet (9 m) and change direction. This helps them to get away safely.

11

Diggers

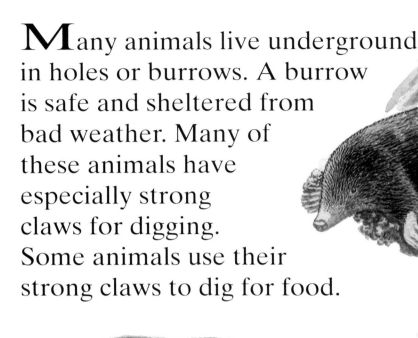

Many animals live underground in holes or burrows. A burrow is safe and sheltered from bad weather. Many of these animals have especially strong claws for digging. Some animals use their strong claws to dig for food.

▲ **Collared Lemming**
The collared lemming lives where winters are cold and snowy. Some of the claws on its front paws grow much larger in winter. The lemming uses these claws to dig through the snow and frozen ground.

12

◄ European Mole

This little mole spends all its life underground. It has large claws on its wide front paws. These help it tunnel through the soil. The mole eats all the creepy crawlies that it finds in its tunnels.

▲ **Alpine Marmot** This small animal spends most of its time underground. It uses the thick claws on its front paws to dig. It makes long tunnels and dens.

◄ **Ratel** This African badger has very long, strong claws on its front paws. It uses them to dig large burrows to sleep in. The badger also climbs and breaks open bees' nests. The ratel is also known as the honey badger.

► Marsupial Mole

The marsupial mole has large front claws. They help the mole to move through sand. It moves as if it were swimming. Then it pushes the sand out of its way with its back paws.

Life at the Top

Lots of animals live in the treetops. These animals have special paws or claws. The claws help them to grip the branches tightly. This means they can move around to find food. They are even able to sleep in the treetops.

▼ **Chameleon** The chameleon does not often leave the safety of the treetops. This lizard grips the branches tightly with its toes.

▲ **Eastern Gray Squirrel** How does this squirrel climb trees so well? It has needle-sharp claws on all its feet. These dig into the tree's rough bark. This way the squirrel never loses its footing.

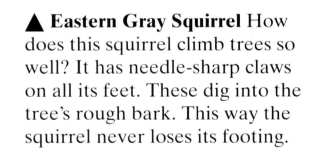

14

▼ **Tree Frog** Tree frogs have large pads on their fingers and toes. The pads are sticky. They help the frog to climb trees and hang beneath leaves.

▶ **Hoatzin** The hoatzin nests in trees that grow in tropical swamps. The young birds climb around in the branches. The young birds have two clawed fingers on each wing. They hook these claws around the branches to keep them from falling.

◀ **White-Handed Gibbon** The gibbon swings through the treetops at full speed. It uses its hands, one after the other, to grip the branches.

Upside-Down

Some animals are very good at holding on tight. They can even climb around when they are upside down. Others have sticky feet! They can walk upside down, too. They can crawl across a ceiling or climb a smooth wall. They never fall off. Their feet keep them safe.

▶ **Three-Toed Sloth** The three-toed sloth has amazing hooked claws 3–4 inches (7–10 cm) long! The grip of the hooks is very strong. The sloth does not even fall off when it dies.

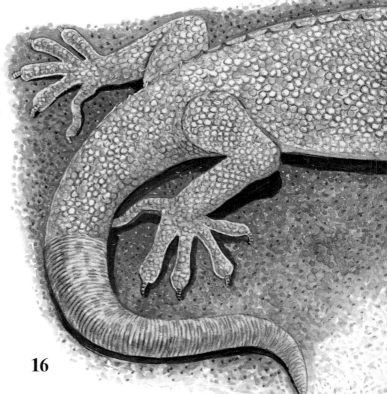

▲ **Bluebottle**
This little fly can walk up panes of glass or across ceilings. It has damp suckers between the tiny claws of each of its six feet. These give the fly a firm grip even on the smoothest surfaces.

▼ Epauletted Fruit Bat The fruit bat only flies around at night. In the daytime it rests in the trees. It hangs upside down on thin branches. There it clings with the hooked claws on its back feet.

▲ Blue-tit The blue-tit curls its toes around a branch and hangs on tight. Each toe has a little claw for extra grip. This little bird can cling upside down on trees or flowers. It finds insects or seeds to eat.

◀ Tockay Gecko Gecko lizards have ridged pads on each toe. These toes get such a good grip that the gecko can climb up trees, rocks, walls — or even windows.

Softly, Softly

Sand and snow are hard to walk on. Animals that live in places with sand or snow have paws that spread out. This keeps them from sinking in.

▼ **Dromedary** The camel lives in the sandy desert. Its large flat feet each have two wide toes. Underneath the camel's feet are flat pads. These keep the camel from sinking into the soft sand.

▶ **Snowshoe Rabbit** The snowshoe rabbit lives in North America, near the Arctic. Its back feet are very wide and furry. They keep the rabbit from sinking into the soft snow. They also keep the rabbit warm.

◀ Jacana The jacana has very long toes, with long straight claws. It spreads its toes wide to run over floating leaves without sinking into the water.

▲ Willow Grouse In the winter, the willow grouse grows thick feathers over its legs and feet. These feathery feet keep it from sinking into the snow.

▼ Web-Footed Gecko Web-footed geckos live in the Namib Desert in Africa. They come out at night to hunt. They scurry around, catching insects to eat. Their webbed toes keep them from sinking into the loose sand.

19

On the Rocks

Many animals live on steep mountains or hills. Their feet are very important. They need to get a good grip. Then they can move around without rolling downhill!

▼ Rock-Hopper Penguin

The rock-hopper penguin may look clumsy. But it leaps over steep, icy rocks with ease. Its wide webbed toes end in claws. This helps it get a firm hold on the slippery frozen ground.

▶ Hermann's Tortoise

Tortoises are slow animals. They cannot leap or jump. Hermann's tortoise pushes its claws into cracks between the rocks to climb around safely.

▼ Rock Hyrax The rock hyrax has moist, rubbery pads on the soles of its feet. This helps the hyrax get a firm grip on the smooth, rocky slopes.

▲ Klipspringer This little antelope leaps across steep rocky slopes on tiptoe. Each hoof has a hard tip and a rubbery pad. These pads keep the antelope from slipping.

▼ Rock Wallaby Most wallabies live on flat grassy plains. Rock wallabies live on hillsides. The soles of their back feet are rough, with little hard lumps. These help them get a solid footing on steep rocks.

21

Handy Hands

You use your hands and fingers to do all kinds of jobs. Some animals use their fingers and paws in almost the same way. A few have even learned to use tools. Others use their front paws to hold their food. Some use their paws to pull food out of difficult places.

▶ **Sea Otter** The sea otter feeds on shellfish. The otter uses a flat stone to break open the shell. This good swimmer floats on its back and rests the stone on its chest. Then it uses its front paws to hit the shellfish on the stone until the shell breaks.

▼ **Giant Panda** The giant panda's wrist bone has grown out to make a false thumb. The panda uses this to help it hold bunches of bamboo stems.

▲ **Chimpanzee** A chimpanzee's hands are somewhat like yours. Some chimps use stones as hammers to crack very hard nuts.

◀ **Aye-Aye** The aye-aye is rare and shy. The third finger on each front paw is very long and thin. It also has a long nail. It uses this finger to pull out insects from small holes under tree bark.

Hunters

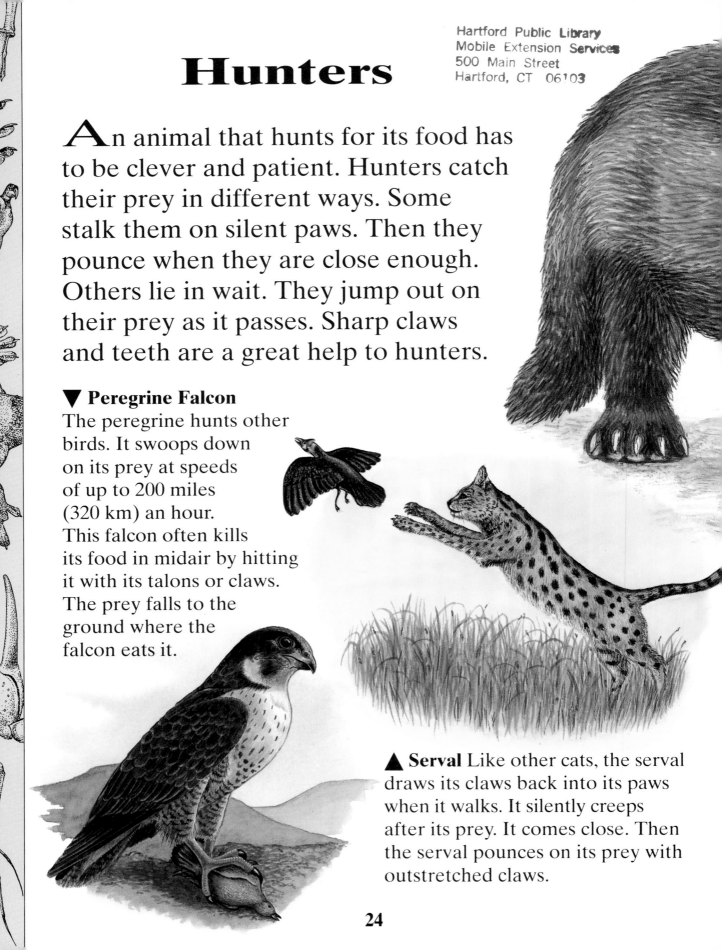

An animal that hunts for its food has to be clever and patient. Hunters catch their prey in different ways. Some stalk them on silent paws. Then they pounce when they are close enough. Others lie in wait. They jump out on their prey as it passes. Sharp claws and teeth are a great help to hunters.

▼ Peregrine Falcon

The peregrine hunts other birds. It swoops down on its prey at speeds of up to 200 miles (320 km) an hour. This falcon often kills its food in midair by hitting it with its talons or claws. The prey falls to the ground where the falcon eats it.

▲ **Serval** Like other cats, the serval draws its claws back into its paws when it walks. It silently creeps after its prey. It comes close. Then the serval pounces on its prey with outstretched claws.

24

◀ Wolverine The wolverine lives in the snowy Arctic. Its big feet help it to walk on soft snow. Each foot has five sharp claws. The wolverine pounces on its prey from trees and rocks. It grips its prey with its strong, sharp claws.

▲ Secretary Bird The secretary bird lives in tall grass. It eats snakes. The bird stamps on the snake with its large feet to kill it. The snake cannot bite the bird's feet because they are very scaly.

◀ Fisherman Bat This fisherman bat flies low over a lake or slow river. When it spots a fish, it snatches it out of the water with the long, curved claws on its back feet.

25

Fight!

Animals do not often fight. If they get badly hurt, they could die. Sometimes animals have to fight. They fight to save their young or themselves from their enemies. Males also fight over females. They may fight to protect their feeding ground. Hard hooves and sharp claws make good weapons.

▼ **Przewalski's Horse** When a horse fights, it rears up on its back legs. It strikes its enemy with its hard front hooves.

▶ **Jungle Fowl** Male jungle fowl fight over females. Males fight each other with sharp claws on their legs, called spurs.

◄ Platypus The male platypus has a secret weapon. On the inside of each back foot is a sharp claw. If a male platypus is attacked, it digs these claws into its rival. It also injects a poison at the same time!

▼ Red Kangaroo Male kangaroos have boxing matches. They hit each other with their front paws. Then they kick out with their back paws.

▼ Edible Crab The front pair of the crab's ten legs ends in huge claws. Crabs use their claws to rip up food. These strong claws can also give an enemy a painful bite.

27

Listen!

Animals of the same kind tell each other many things. They cannot speak to each other as we do. They use their voices to call to each other. They also use their paws and claws to send messages. Animals that live in groups often send warnings if they are in danger. Animals that live alone leave signs of where they are. Pairs of animals "talk" to each other to stay together.

▼ **Blue-Footed Booby** Male and female blue-footed boobies do a "dance" to stay together. Each bird lifts and holds up one bright blue foot after the other.

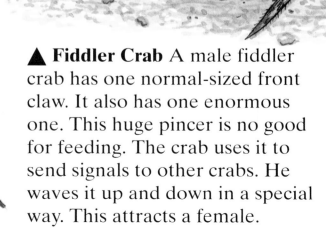

▲ **Fiddler Crab** A male fiddler crab has one normal-sized front claw. It also has one enormous one. This huge pincer is no good for feeding. The crab uses it to send signals to other crabs. He waves it up and down in a special way. This attracts a female.

▶ Mongolian Gerbil

Gerbils live in family groups. If danger threatens, one of them thumps the ground with its hind feet. This thumping makes a drumming sound that warns the other gerbils.

▲ Gorilla

The head of a gorilla's family group is a silverback male. Sometimes he thumps his chest with his hands. This tells other male gorillas how important he is.

▶ Black Bear

A male black bear keeps his territory for himself. He makes deep, long scratches on tree trunks with his front claws. This lets other bears know that this area is his home.

Swimmers

Most birds and four-legged animals live and feed on land. But seas, ponds, and rivers are full of food! Some mammals and birds have learned how to swim well. Their paws have changed to help them to move through the water. Some swimming animals have webbed paws. Animals that live in the water no longer have paws. They have flippers instead. Some of these animals cannot walk on land at all anymore.

▶ **Common Seal** Seals use their back flippers when they swim. On shore, they support themselves on their front flippers. They move by wiggling over the ground.

▲ **Atlantic Whiteside Dolphin** The dolphin has no back legs or paws at all! They have vanished. Its front "paws" are flippers. The dolphin swims with its front flippers and tail fins. It does not come ashore. If it gets washed on to the shore, it cannot move at all.

▼ Californian Sea Lion

This sea lion spends a lot of time in the sea. It uses its strong front flippers to swim. On shore, the sea lion walks using its front and back flippers.

▼ Eurasian Water Shrew

The water shrew lives in holes that it makes in riverbanks. It dives into the water to catch its prey. The shrew's back feet are webbed and fringed to help it swim.

▲ Mute Swan

Swans have large webbed feet. Swans use these feet to paddle along in the water. These feet are also used as brakes when the swan lands on the water.

In for the Kill

Some animals have truly scary claws. The rest of the animal is often pretty big as well. These are the largest hunters.

▶ **Harpy Eagle** The harpy eagle is the most powerful bird of prey in the world. Each foot can spread out to nearly 10 inches (25 cm). Its talons, or claws, are 1½ inches (about 4 cm) long. No wonder monkeys and sloths are scared of them.

◀ **Polar Bear** The polar bear is the largest meat-eating animal in the world! It uses its powerful paws and claws to catch seals.

▶ **Tiger** This tiger is the largest animal in the cat family. The tiger has big, strong paws armed with sharp claws. It is a fierce hunter.

32

▼ **Cassowary** A cassowary is a large, fierce bird. It cannot fly, but it can run fast on its strong, thick legs. Cassowaries will even attack people. They lash out with their feet. They slash an enemy with their big claws.

▼ **Baryonyx** Baryonyx is an extinct reptile. One finger on each front foot had a claw 6 inches (15 cm) long. Baryonyx probably used this claw to catch fish.

Quiz

1. How does the marsupial mole move through the sand?

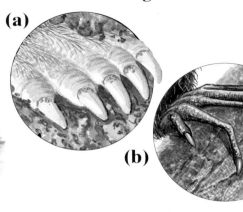

2. What does a dolphin have instead of legs?

3. How does the Mongolian gerbil warn of danger?

4. Which animals do these paws and claws belong to?

(a)

(b)

5. How does a garden spider hold on to her web?

6. What are these baboons doing?

7. Why are squirrels such good climbers?

8. How does the secretary bird kill snakes?

9. Which animals do these claws belong to?

(a)

(b)

10. Why does the willow grouse have feathery feet?

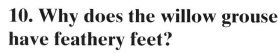

11. How does the sloth hang upside down?

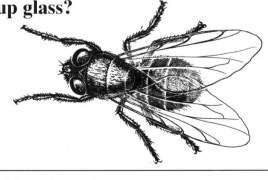

12. Why can a bluebottle walk up glass?

If you do not know the answers turn to the following pages:
1. p13, **2.** p30, **3.** p29, **4a.** p13, **4b.** p23,
5. p9, **6.** p6, **7.** p14, **8.** p25, **9a.** p32,
9b. p19, **10.** p19, **11.** p16, **12.** p16

Glossary

Bamboo A kind of grass that has hard, woody stems. Bamboo is the largest of grasses.

Bark The tough, outer covering of the woody parts of a tree. Bark helps to keep insects and other pests from damaging the tree.

Burrow A large tunnel that many kinds of animals dig in the ground. Some animals live in their burrows. Others just use them to sleep in or to make nests for their young. Sometimes they dig burrows to find food.

Den A hole in a burrow, a cave, or a similar place where an animal rests and sleeps. Sometimes animals raise their young in a den.

Desert A part of the world where rain hardly ever falls. Little grows in the desert.

Fleas Small insects that live on warm-blooded animals and feed on their blood.

Flippers The wide, flat limb of an animal that is used for swimming. This kind of animal spends most, or all, of its time in the water.

Frog An animal with a wide mouth, small front legs, very large back legs, and no tail. The frog has smooth, moist skin. A frog lives part of its life in water and part of its life on land. Frogs belong to the group of animals called amphibians.

Herd A large group of animals of one kind. These often graze, or feed, together.

Hoof The thick, horny covering of the foot of some animals, such as horses. Hoofed animals can run for long distances over hard ground. Their hooves protect the softer parts of their feet.

Insect A small animal with six legs. The adult form has a hard case around its body. Most insects have two or four wings.

Lizard A cold-blooded animal with a scaly skin. Lizards belong to a group of animals called reptiles.

Predator An animal that kills and eats other animals.

Prey An animal that is killed and eaten by another animal.

Seed A small, dry object made by a flowering plant. Under the right conditions, seeds will sprout and grow into new plants.

Shell The hard, chalky layer that covers some kinds of soft-bodied animals.

Shellfish A soft-bodied sea animal that has a hard, chalky shell.

Silk The thin, tough threads that a spider spins and makes into a web.

Silverback The male gorilla at the head of a family group. His shoulders and back are covered with silvery gray hairs.

Swamps Large areas of land that are always covered with still, shallow water. Swamps usually have special kinds of trees growing in them.

Talons The very large, sharp claws that birds of prey and owls have on their feet.

Termites These antlike insects often live in the tropics. They live in colonies and in huge nests. Each colony may contain thousands of termites. They live in large mounds that they build with mud mixed with saliva (spit).

Tool Some object that an animal uses to do a task that it cannot do just by using its body.

Web The mesh of silk threads that a spider builds to trap insects.

Webbed feet Feet or paws where the fingers or toes are joined by a thin layer of skin.

Index

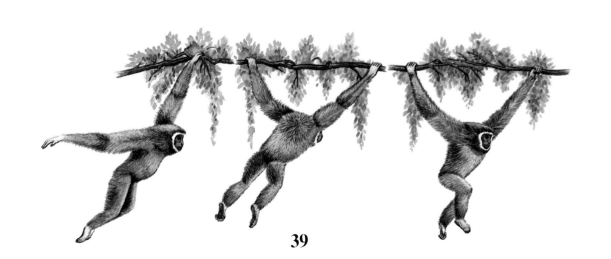

A TEMPLAR BOOK

Devised and produced by The Templar Company plc
Pippbrook Mill, London Road, Dorking,
Surrey RH4 1JE, Great Britain

MOBILE EXTENSION
Date Due